Rishtey Kucch Apne Se

Sweetness Sourness and Bitterness of a Relationship

Anuj Kumar Rajan

Made with ❤ on the BookLeaf Publishing Platform
www.bookleafpub.in
www.bookleafpub.com

Dedication

I dedicate my book to my mother, who has devoted herself to us and taught me invaluable lessons. She showed me that we should forget the pain of giving without expecting anything in return, reminding me that relationships aren't transactions. Happiness comes from making our loved ones smile.

This book is also dedicated to those who have briefly crossed my path and imparted life's lessons. I've encountered friends and foes, supporters and deceivers, those who have loved me and those who have challenged me. Each person has played a role in shaping my journey, whether through kindness or hardship.

To everyone who has touched my life, in ways both good and bad, I dedicate this book. It embodies the essence of "Rishey Kucch Apne Se"—the connections we nurture and the relationships we navigate.

Preface

Relationships are at the core of what it means to be human. We are born around them, shaped by them, and inevitably, we search for meaning within them. Whether it's the bond between parent and child, the connection between friends, or the intricate dance of romantic love, relationships form the threads that weave the fabric of our lives. They bring us joy and fulfillment, but they also challenge us, sometimes breaking us only to rebuild us stronger and wiser.

This book is a journey through the many facets of relationships—the love that elevates us, the conflicts that test us, and the moments of vulnerability that bind us to others. It is not just a story, but an exploration of the highs and lows, the beginnings and endings, the lessons learned and unlearned. Through each chapter, I hope to offer a glimpse into the complexities of human connection, from the tender to the turbulent, and everything in between.

We often seek out others to fill the gaps within us, but in truth, the most profound relationships are those that challenge us to grow, to evolve, and to understand ourselves more deeply. In these pages, you will find reflections on intimacy, trust, communication, and the delicate balance between independence and togetherness.

It is my hope that this book will resonate with anyone who has ever loved, lost, or yearned to understand what it truly means to connect with another person. For relationships, in all their forms, are not only the mirror through which we see each other, but also the mirror in which we see ourselves.

Welcome to this exploration of the heart—the messy, beautiful, and transformative journey of being truly connected.

Acknowledgements

Writing a poem about relationships is, in many ways, like building one: it requires the support, patience, and understanding of many people. This project has been an exploration not only of my own experiences but of the wisdom, love, and insights that others have shared with me along the way. Without these individuals, this book would not have come into being.

First and foremost, I owe a debt of gratitude to my family. To my parents, whose love taught me the importance of vulnerability, communication, and commitment—your example has been my greatest guide. To my siblings and extended family, whose unwavering support and encouragement have been my constant source of strength—thank you for reminding me, often without words, that I am never truly alone. Love of my life, who taught me the purpose of my life and gave me a reason to survive.

To my friends, whose shared laughter, shared tears, and deep conversations have illuminated the complexities of human connection: you have all shaped this book in ways too numerous to name. The truth of our relationships has grounded me, and your authenticity has given me the courage to explore the sometimes uncomfortable, yet necessary, truths about intimacy, love, and conflict.

Every story, every heartbreak, every triumph has added depth and nuance to my understanding of what it means to love and be loved. I am honored by your trust.

A special thank you goes to BookLeaf Publishing for allowing me to share my thought to the public where they can relate it with their own real world and enjoy the nuances of each relationship around them.

And lastly, to the people who read these words: I hope that through this book, you will find a reflection of your own experiences, or perhaps gain a new perspective on the relationships in your life. Relationships are never perfect, but they are the mirror through which we understand ourselves. Thank you for allowing me to explore these reflections with you.
This book is a testament to the connections that shape us, and I am grateful to everyone who has touched my life, directly or indirectly, on this journey.

With deep appreciation,
Anuj

1. मां

वो मुझे मुस्कुराते देख तेरा मुस्कुराना,
खुद के आंसू को छुपा के मुझे खेलाना,
याद आ जाता है मुझे हर पल
रात में बंद आँखों के साथ भी तेरा मुझे सुलाना।

खुद को भूखे रख के मुझे खिलाना,
अपनी बीमारी में भी मुझे रोने से चुप कराना,
अपने झगड़ों को मेरी आँखों में भूल जाना
याद आता है मुझे हर पल
लोगो की परवाह किये बिना तेरा मुझे दूध पिलाना।

वो खुद बिखरे रह मुझे सजाना संवारना,
खुद घुटने पे रह मुझे अपनी अंगुली पकड़ के चलाना,
खुद को तकलीफ़ में रख मुझे हर तकलीफ़ से बचाना,
हर पल याद आता है मुझे
खुद को गिरते पड़ते छोड़ मुझे सही राह दिखाना।

आज जो भी हम हैं और जो है वजूद है हमारा,
ये कुछ नहीं बस दुआ और प्यार है तुम्हारा,
माँ बच्चे का रिश्ता है सारे रिश्तों से न्यारा,

याद आता है मुझे हर पल
मेरी शरारतों को भूल मुझे हर पल गले लगाना।

मेरी हर सांसे तेरा नाम है मेरी माँ,
अगर मैं जी भी रहा हूं तो तेरी दुआ मेरे साथ है मेरी मां,
मैं तुझे एक पल भूल भी गया तो ये गुनाह है मेरी माँ।
जब तक सांसे रहेगी मैं तुझे प्यार करता रहूंगा मेरी मां।

2. Mother my god

Whenever I try to see in my memory lane.
Near or far I can see only one woman.

This woman is near me whatever and whenever I need.
This woman is teaching me what is a good or a bad deed.

She was my support when I was not able to walk.
She was my voice when I was not able to talk.

Standing behind me whenever I was crying.
But not to show her tears that she was always trying.

My teacher, my guide, my friend, my parents and many
roles did she play.
Stopping her all work and desire to fulfil my needs
without any delay.

The entire childhood we spent with the help of only one
rope.
Whenever we are down that woman always show us ray

of hope.

Now when we are matured and grown so old.
How can we forget her and how can we forget whatever
she told.

I do not have words to describe her anymore.
How can a sea describe the role of the shore.

Whenever in our memory lane we see any day.
We find that it is you only my dear mom that I can pray.

3. Learning Curve

Nobody born in the earth with relation or with any
greed.
This world teaches them the role of a family and what
we need.

We enjoy cherishing our moment, we start growing and
growing our needs.
We start following the path that they make us to follow,
and it becomes guiding factor of our deeds.

By the time we grow older we learn so many tricks.
Because then we find ourselves broken multiple times
without using any solid brick.

We realize that everybody is fulfilling their needs with
without giving any value to relation.
People are smiling with you with pain in their heart and
with no good intention.

By the time we understand that so many smiles and

relations were fake.

We find ourselves as a part of game, it is already too late.

Most of us have so many friends but from inside we feel
lonely and wanted to cry.

But now in front of this world our tears do not want to
flow and I do not even try.

We keep on thinking our situation and look for someone
to blame.

Because we have already wasted our life by being part of
this worldly game.

4. रिश्तों का चौकीदार

एक समय हमारा दोस्त रिश्तों का चौकीदार था।
सब कुछ मुझसे ले लेता पर क्या हुआ वो तो मेरा यार था।

उसके कारण ही तो सारे रिश्ते थे मेरे जूड़े।
उसके लिए तो मैंने अपने सपनों के किए टुकड़े।

वो मुस्कुराता तो सोचता कितना खुश है रिश्ते मेरे।
वो रोता तो गिनाता क्या अभी और होने है टुकड़े मेरे।

शायद एक दिन मैं थक गया और ना मिल पाया चौकीदार से।
उस दिन से वो रूठ गया और ना मिलने दिया मेरे किसी भी प्यार से।

फिर तो ना बचे रिश्ते और बच गए मेरे दुखड़े।
चौकीदार हंसा उन दुखड़ो पे और फिर से मैं गिना रह गया मेरे टुकड़े।

5. Friends Forever

Hey, do you remember me pulling your leg to make you
smile?
Do you know, with me you have stayed for a long while?

I am there with you in each phase of your life.
May be my face has changed but always stayed with if it
is a day or night.

At times I am your family your advisor and your guide.
But I am there with you whenever your life is in a rough
ride.

I always enjoyed the food after stealing it from your
tiffin.
Because more than anything I also loved your teasing.

We have shared our feelings and set our trends.
Because we are together as we are the best friends.

6. Purpose of Life

Most of us are sad and struggling with our own life.
As without knowing the actual purpose, we want to
achieve great height.

We are not even interested in knowing the reason of our
life and waste it only in show off.
By the time we actually realize, we find that our life is
already a joke.

We like to complain about life, and we find it so
complicated.
But we never plan to make it simple, and we love to call
it sophisticated.

We keep showing ourselves better keep proving that we
have so much empathy.
But actually, when we realize then we know how much
actually we need sympathy.

We keep trying for something that we actually do not

need.
At the end we lost our whole life just to fulfil our greed.

Finally, we realize that we have nothing, and the purpose
of life is lost.
We actually did not care for ourselves when it was
needed most.

The day we will realize the actual reason and purpose for
our life.
We will stop struggling unnecessarily and then able to
see our and make others future bright.

7. Society vs Goal

There was a sleepless night making me worried for my
life.
I was feeling like all of my relationship was on knife.

I was confused, what to do and whom to follow.
I was getting hiccups as it was very hard to swallow.

Relations were worried about my body my wealth but
killing my soul.
Had to choose between the relation and enjoying the real
goal.

I tried my best to keep both my body and soul alive.
But got tired by handling the pressure of real-world life.

Finally, I decided to follow the world and kill the soul.
To match with the world where people have killed their
soul with no real goal.

At least now they see me smiling like everyone smiles.

But who cares if there is a real happiness in the heart
even for a short while.

12

8. The Real Goal

We will feel very happy when we start our career.
We feel proud of ourselves and think that we did break
the barrier.

We love to see numbers coming in our bank account.
And we are so busy in that we forget our relationship
count.

Sooner or later, we realize the fact and start getting tired.
As most of us never decide where we should get hired.

So many of us go for money and forget our passion.
Then why we think what went wrong and why there is
so much of tension.

We lose our identity, family, friends and health.
Because we do not care about them, and we run only the
wealth.

We acquire ego, anger along with luxury and our greed

is always on

But we do not even realize where the value of life has gone.

Hope we will start realizing who are our best mate. Before we became a machine, and emotion finds it too late.

9. Virtual Friends

One day I was showing someone the number of my
online friends.
I was feeling so proud and as I was just following the
latest trend.

Then he asked me how many of them that I have actually
meet.
How many of them have time for me and did we
together seat?

I have started counting and realized that there are not so
many.
And when I have to find a real friend then I can hardly
find any.

It seems we are so happy and so much busy in the virtual
world.
We forget our actual friends and relatives that are in real
world.

I was replying to my virtual world and forgot to say my
real friends "Hi".
I was too busy chatting with them I did not even listen
when my close ones left me saying "Bye".

Now when I am looking at me and realized that I have
no one and I am so alone.
I have some smile, but my real happiness seems like
already gone.

10. जिंदगी

मैंने जिंदगी से पूछा तुम क्यों मुझे इतना सताती हो।
हर पल यू मुझे क्यू इतना रुलाती हो।

जिंदगी बोली कहा मैं तुझे सताती हूँ।
मैं तो हमेशा तुझे जीने का मतलब सिखाती हूँ।

तुझे क्यों लगता है कि मैं तुझे हर पल रुलाती हूं।
अरे जब रोते हो तो हंसने का मजा भी तो बताती हो।

फिर भूख नहीं तो खाने का क्या मजा है।
पीना प्यासा तो पानी पीना भी एक सजा है।

गम के बाद ही तो ख़ुशी का मजा देती है जिंदगी।
अपनों के होने और खोने का एहसास देती है जिंदगी।

ख़ुशी में सारे लोग अच्छे दिखते हैं तुम्हें
पर गम में अपनों की परख करती है जिंदगी।

गम नहीं तो फिर कोरा है हर ख़ुशी का हर एहसास।
बहुत कम लोग होते हैं जिन्हे जिंदगी का सच्चा मिलता है साथ।

11. Finding God

I was wondering that despite so many prayers why we
cannot see the God?
We follow so much of custom but still why cannot we
speak with the Lord?

May be there were some problems in our prayers in
keeping our God happy.
May be there were some problems with me, and I am
being too sloppy.

Do we know our relationship with the God, or it is just
an ignorance?
Do we know how beautiful it is when devotion starts
spreading its own fragrance?

Do we know that what the God is looking for, how can
we become their dear?
If we have done nothing wrong, then why there should
be any kind of fear?

It seems like we are too busy in following the custom
rather actually serving the God.
We do not have anything to give to them, but we need
everything from our super Lord.

God is everything for us and we consider them as a
friend, relatives and our parents
When we are with God then why cannot enjoy our
relationship and enjoy the moments.

We know it well that we need to have a passion and love
if we want something in our life
Then cannot we offer our unconditional love to get
someone who is actually our life.

The day we will start praying the God unconditionally
with no more greed.
God will come looking for you as they need you more
than what you need.

12. खुद से प्यार

आज फिर से मुझे खुद से प्यार हो गया है।
मेरा मुझपे अपना अधिकार हो गया है।

मोह माया के बंधनो को छोड़ के।
मेरा दिल मेरा हाय यार हो गया है।

कोशिश की रिश्तों को बहुत निभाने की।
झूठी हंसी के सहारे अपने आंसू को छुपाने की।

झूठे तस्सलियो के सहारे सच्चा प्यार पाने की।
सबके दर्द में अपने दर्द को भूल जाने की।

थक गया ये दिल और ठहर सी गई जिंदगी।
रो रो के तो अब तो आंसू भी मेरी थम गई।

भावनाएं सारी कहीं कोने में जम गई।
रिश्तों में भरोसा करके मेरी जिंदगी ही कम गई।

अब तो मैं फिर से बेफिक्र रहने को तैयार हो गया।
जो दर्द था वो सब मेरा यार हो गया।

मैं फिर से खुश रहने को तैयार हो गया।
मुझे तो आज अपने आप से प्यार हो गया।

13. Our Parents

Everytime when I woke up at night, I find that I am so
alone.
I do have everything, but somewhere real happiness has
gone.

I always prioritize my aim, and my requirements made
me so needy.
To fulfil my need, I forget my surroundings; my relations
and I became so greedy.

I left everyone in a search of my dream and make my
own world.
Real world is made of love, but it was too late by the
time I have learned.

When I turn back, now I realized that I have always
ignored tears in someone eyes.
My parents were waiting and praying for me always
looking at sky.

They were the one who sacrificed their life to help me
achieve my aim.
Without expecting anything for them as I am their only
gem.

I grow with their unlimited love, and they were my only
rope.
But where I am when they are in need, and I am their
only hope.

Thanks to you mom and dad for making me achieve my
dream
And sorry as I realized that with my selfishness I
became so mean.

How can forget you in my prayer how can I forget what
you did.
Why I am so far from you why I am not there when you
need.

Still when I wake up, I find that I am so alone.
Without my mom and dad my somewhere my real
happiness has gone.

14. Teacher

We should not forget the person who made our base.
Who taught as to fight and win all the race.

From outside they always appear very strong and very
tough.
But they appear like this so that our life will not become
rough.

We never know how deep rooted they are in their
thoughts.
Surprisingly we only remember when they used to
shout.

They spend their all-time to shape our life.
Then how come we can forget their sacrifice.

We should not forget we are good because our teachers
were great.
We should always pray for them and give them a due
respect.

15. The walk on the seashore

I love to walk on the seashore alone.
It reminds me of all days that are gone.

I feel so silent even if the waves try to make some sound.
Because feeling is so deep inside and in it, I am so
drowned.

While walking along the seashore I feel so calm.
As if somebody is healing my pain by applying some
balm.

It takes me to the memory lane of my life that I travelled
all alone.
I can freely roll out my tears remembering all the good
vibes that are gone.

Then I smile looking at the long and long seashore.
I return back thinking about the bright future coming
along.

Waves gives me a courage to live a new life again.
As old waves break after hitting to shore just to go back
and became stronger again.

16. अजनबी रिश्ते

चलते-चलते रहो मुझे कोई अजनबी मिल जाता है।
उनसे बहुत कम है जो दिल के करीब आते हैं।

उनसे हमारे दिलो के अजीब रिश्ते जुड़ जाते हैं।
दर्द बहुत होता जब वो फिर अजनबी बन जाता।

अब तो हम किसी अजनबी को देख ही डर जाते हैं।
पास आने के नाम से ही आंसू से भर जाते हैं।

अब तो सोचता हूँ किसी की यादों में क्यूँ खुद को सताता है।
चलो सबको छोड़ सारे रिश्ते से अजनबी बन जाते हैं।

17. The Father

I smile with my family and hiding my all pain.
I sacrifice my life for kids without expecting any gain.

I am standing and saving them from all issues if it is
winter summer or rain.
I am doing all for them whatever I can.

Everybody finds me too tough to break with hurdles.
But I can cry easily whenever I hug my kids and
whenever I cuddle.

I have to stay tough so that I can take all the pain.
Because I can still smile as my family's happiness is my
biggest gain.

I am your support, your protector, your roof, I am your
dad.
Who just live for his kids and any issues with them can
only make me sad.

18. God's best creation- A woman

While God were creating the earth they left with some
hidden treasure.
They wanted to give some best of this to the best ever
creature.

Then they have decided to create the woman.
Who can protect their family and support all the human.

Who can give unlimited love without expectation.
But at the same time, she can kill the demon without
hesitation.

At the same she can play different roles of a mom, a wife,
a sister and a daughter.
With no excuses and new battlefields, she always proves
herself as a great fighter.

Such a beautiful creature of God needs only respect and
some care.

But never consider them weak and disrespecting her do not even dare.

19. Tough choice

I was crying and trying to be tough.
But I am tired now and already had enough.

When we have to choose and take strong decisions.
We find ourselves in front of the god asking for the
solution.

From the life I get love and from the love I get life.
I was confused if without love there will be any meaning
of life.

Nevertheless, to avoid complications, I have chosen to
live without my life.
Now, I have tears as my only love, and I am living this
never-ending sacrifice.

It would have been different if I had chosen my love and
to live with my life.
I would have just sacrificed some ego but would have
been enjoying my life.

20. Strange expectations

Human beings are such a fool creature by their own
emotions.
They do not think much before creating any connections.

They grow old, always surrounded with their relations.
Which makes them happy and but then they create so
much of expectations.

We do not realize that our relations will leave us one day
leaving all artificial creations.
Once they leave us, we find ourselves getting fooled
again with our own emotions.

We find that only we left with memory and tears in our
eyes.
It is our own who leave us always, whatever we can try.

21. खामोश रिश्ते

बहुत पुकारा उन रिश्तों ने इसे पहले कि वो पकड़े खामोशियों का
सहारा।
कहीं दूर चल गए हमें छोड़ भूल के, शायद वही तो हमारा सहारा।

बोलना चाहता भी हूं तो भी शायद अब मेरी आवाज नहीं पहुंचेगी
उनके पास।
क्योंकि खामोश करके रिश्तों को वो तो छोड़ बैठे हैं मेरा साथ।

शायद पूछते हैं हमसे कहा था तुम जब हमने तुम्हें पुकारा।
वो भूल जाते हैं कि निभाना बहुत चाहा हमने परिस्थितियो के बावजूद
पर हमें छोड़ गए वो किनारा।

अब मिलते भी हैं तो अंजान से जैसे हम कभी नहीं थे एक दूजे का
सहारा।
खामोश रिश्तों के इस दर्द को शायद वापस बयान कर पाता कभी
दोबारा।